Wonderstand

Sohan Qadri

The pictures on the front page and on pages 8, 53 and 61 are from paintings by *Sohan Qadri*.

The photografic portrait of *Sohan Qadri* is by *Swami Janakananda.*

•

The Dot and the dots was first published in Danish in the magazine *Bindu* 1975.

The book as a whole was first published in English by *Writer's Workshop Publications*, Calcutta, India. 1988.

In 1995 it was published in Danish and English together by *Ørnens Forlag,* Denmark.

•

2009 *Bindu Publishers*
International Haa Course Center
34013 Hamneda Sweden
www.bindu.eu

printed in Sweden at
Joma Grafisk Produktion AB, Ljungby,
the insert on the paper *Lessebo Linné*
and the cover on *Invercote G*

ISBN: 978-91-977894-0-0

Wonderstand

•

Aphorisms

•

The Dot
and
the Dots

•

Sohan Qadri

•

bindu

Content:

Foreword

What is the purpose of true art and literature? It is to make us see – to experience ourselves and the universe in which we are living. To be present where we are and in what we do.

The aboriginal of Australia, when he lies down in the landscape, he expands his consciousness through being one with and 'seeing' the landscape he is in – with its pathways, and the positions of waterholes, animals and people.

Sohan Qadri's poems or aphorisms are in line with a similar original tradition, the tantric tradition of India. Sohan's guru was a tantric, whom he met as a child. He grew up in that tradition in a small village in Punjab.

The word *tan-tra* originally means *to expand* and through that expansion *to liberate*. When you expand your consciousness there can be no limitations such as taste or judgement. Everything there is, is part of the experience and part of you.

The poems of Sohan Qadri show us that 'dot' of consciousness, *bindu*, which is present everywhere, without discrimination, in every thing and every one – you realise your self through *any*thing.

In the song *Tantric Devi Suktam* the goddess is defined by everything there is: consciousness, reason, sleep, hunger, shadow, energy, thirst, bashfullnes, delusion, vocation ...

That power who exists in all beings as vocation
reverence to her, reverence to her,
reverence to her, reverence, reverence.

In *The Dot and the dots* Sohan carries on that tradition, expanding our minds by placing the dot everywhere, among the lips of lovers, in the northern lights, among the galaxies, and yet we remain right here.

i am a dot
in the orgiastic ecstasy
so spiritual
and so mundane
at once (p. 60)

But you don´t have to know the secrets of Tantra to experience his poems – they will inspire you and convey its universal message anyway.

There is a connection from *Vigyana Bhairava Tantra* 4000 years back in time ...

Sweet-hearted one, meditate on knowing and not knowing, existing and not existing. Then leave both aside that you may ***be***

... to Sohan today.

You ***are***
not because of
what you ***are not****,*
you simply ***are****.*
this simple of you
is the whole
of the whole,
sense it
beyond senses. (p. 41)

This to me is reason enough to publish these poems again – there may be more, but that is for the reader to discover.

Swami Janakananda
Copenhagen 2009

There is no person or place
in these passing shadows.
I may be read and recognized
as you, he, she, it.
Words are only shadows,
seeking the taintless surface
of awareness.

S. Q.

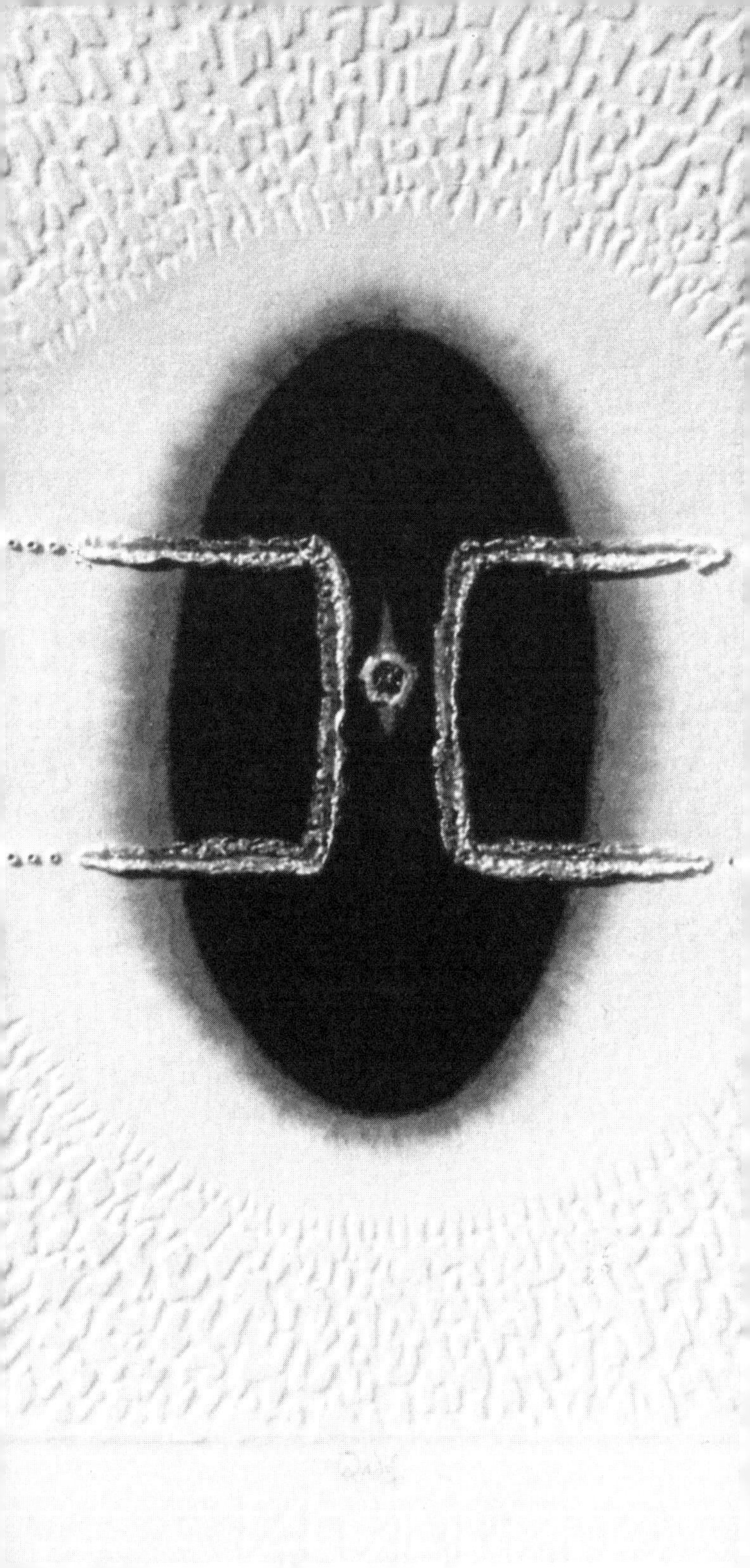

The Line
is the foot-prints
of the Dot
on the face
of the space.

• •

Art – ist
a total surrender
to the brush
with all the paraphernalia –
ever possessed –
and homage to the canvas.

• •

The Reality
can only be –
in the subjectivity,
all objectivity obliterates.

• •

In the becoming
rules forgetfulness,
in the being
just remembrance.

• •

The desire takes
a thousand faces,
all justification
lacks legs.

• •

By losing the left and the right,
the loser neither
falls left nor right
– nor in the middle,
there's left no place to fall
– no need to rise.

• •

In the rising
by the same,
by which one falls –
one never falls again.

• •

In the loss of longing
belonging gets lost –
hence emancipation.

• •

The meditation flowers
as mentation withers.

• •

Boons received in sleep
the recipient
dreams in the dream,
for dream
is the only bud of sleep.

• •

All the events of life
are sequential
hence consequential –
Life is not.

• •

Living hangs mechanically
between two habits
birth and death,
but Life *ad infinitum*.

• •

Intellect is male
intuition is female,
the mystery cannot be solved,
it can only be lived.

• •

The moment is missed
from moment to moment.

• •

Name your own name:
to begin with if you can –
then the name of the game
then play – if you can.

• •

In the kiss
of fire and water
the naked drop dances
while the song
of rain is born.

• •

The seed dies
into the first root
and the first shoot –
to be born again.

• •

The answer dances
when the questioner dies
in the question.

• •

In the kiss of bliss
all lips part – depart.

• •

For the winner:
something remains unwon
the game goes on;
for the loser
nothing left to lose,
the game is lost –
hence freedom.

• •

Success is scaled
in two,
happiness blooms
in one. . .

• •

I tread ahead of me
or I am perfectly still,
every scene seems seen,
every touch feels felt,
every moment looks lived,
in the mindfulness
»Satori« comes not
neither it goes.

• •

One and the same
aloneness dances
in all togetherness.

• •

All offerings are availed
only by being available
– without armour –
present to the present
bliss happens
in the vulnerability.

• •

The question is one
answers many –
move your move, let's play.
the health is one
diseases many
show your card let's play.

• •

When the right ear gets
what is whispered in the left,
the revelation is revealed
in the *Chidakash*.

• •

All goings, all comings
will go on taking away
from the threshold of the home,
so watch, wait and stay.

• •

All choice is partial,
in the whole
the chooser is contained.

• •

In the known
thoughts move,
doubt persists
– hence debate,
in the unknown
thoughts die, doubt dissolves
– hence silence.

• •

To say *neti, neti*
is to say *asti, asti,*
the sayer soils the saying.

• •

All effort hangs on hope,
all hope hangs in the future
– loses Now –
hence new effort, new hope,
while nothing is new
under the sun.

• •

With inward rising
all else is raised,
skies are reached;
with outward rising
all else is demeaned,
hypocrisy is preached.

• •

The obvious absurd
is robed
in a thousand colours,
while the purity
is disrobed
in the wakeful ecstasy
of this obvious absurd,
where else?

• •

The feet following
their own footprints
retreat to reach
the goal within.

• •

The heart throbs
in this bosom,
in the total embrace
the *immediate* melts
while the *ultimate*
is embraced

• •

The wayfarer
is the only way,
the source being
the only goal.

• •

While digging deep
to bury the obvious
the mysterious
is dug out.

• •

The profane
mirrors the profound
only reversed –
wonderstanding
the dynamics
one is at home.

• •

The solitudes
people the pilgrimage
to the hermitage
to celebrate the solitude
in the multitude.

• •

The word is easily reached
though all approach
is partial,
the Whole dawns upon one
that is none.

• •

Nobody's space
is the abode
in the gap –
between galaxies.

• •

The white canary sings
knowing not how
the listener is taught,
no parting is sorrow
if meeting is joy.

• •

In the desert-dream
dunes dwell
yet dwell not,
only a grain of sand
seeks to *wonderstand.*

• •

In agony and ecstasy
ripens Reality,
so let loose the dance.

• •

The Truth
cast into idea
loses its truth,
the mould takes hold.

• •

The thought
is a longing –
while thoughts
become things
– hence belonging.

• •

The only courage is
to watch and witness
the false face fall.

• •

While *one* enters
the *other* exits,
the door is one
and the same.

• •

Know thy feet twice,
retreat a step –
to know thyself.

• •

In falling short
of all the answers
the question
falls apart.

• •

By letting it be
the silence hampers
the thunder down,
and raises the whisper up.

• •

The miser lives misery
the generous tiptoe
hingeing upon the other,
call, need and the needy
say, greed and the greedy.

• •

The higher the profile
the heavier the support,
the lower lives light.

• •

Black and white
interplay –
the grey conspiracy
a harmony.

• •

The divine
and devil
meet and merge
in the marrow:
the grey-matter.

• •

Only the indulger knows
the wetness of water
everybody fasts
between meals.

• •

Carrying bottomless bowls
the silence and sound dance,
the music is poured,
eh! pours the music.

• •

Two can only collide
the harmony –
remains in the making
but merging –
just awaiting.

• •

The two are two
because of the One
hidden between.

• •

In the choosing
the chooser devides
hence gets devided.

• •

All the thoughts,
words and deeds
remain other-oriented,
the split sustains.

• •

To be freed!
the beast begins to bark,
to be cultured!
the face becomes false,
next to none
be done to one,
save metamorphosis.

• •

My God! barks the dog
to shut up the man,
who keeps on barking
in silence and sleep.

• •

With all its
agony and ecstasy
in the harlot' s bed,
celibacy is born.

• •

Let me go far
to come near,
perhaps he said;
there is no far
which is not near,
perhaps she said.

• •

In the language of more
nothing is enough
and the more
becomes a burden.

• •

The Himalaya is lost
behind a speck of dust
in the eye.

• •

My heart belongs to daddy
and mind to great granny,
body borrowed from
elements,
beyond belonging a Swami.

• •

Wait and See, a rare key:
the river flows, grass grows,
responds the pond
the mud settles, one can see.

• •

In a million of modes
everything moves
into everything else,
the gaps becomes bridges.

• •

The matter is Life
divided into parts,
the parts put together
never make the Whole.

• •

Letting the stranger be
in the friend,
and vice versa
the relation falls fit.

• •

In Essence, two are One,
in Existence, two embrace,
in embrace, Essence again,
One is awake two asleep.

• •

The only way
to climb the peak,
– relax in the valley;
the only way
to drink in the ocean
– drown in the ocean.

• •

While a glance
grows into a gaze
the gestalt deepens
a glimpse glistens.

• •

Darkness is invisible
So is Light,
only things unseen,
now are seen,
the seer remains unseen.

• •

One-half runs from sorrow
the other runs to happiness,
in staying
stays the whole.

• •

The doer is doomed
in trying to fill
the inverted pot,
the earth knows better.

• •

Before desiring
how one can know?
before knowing
how one can say?
after, spreads silence.

• •

The shores, river apart
deep down heart to heart
shake hands, touch toes,
in the lap the river flows.

• •

Following fireflies
– running in the dark
all in search of
the blown out flame
. . . all in vain.

• •

The low-lying ocean
hosts the great river
with memories
of the mountains,
with murmurs of the wind,
and whispers and secrets
of the valley,
– no obligation.

• •

The art of enjoying
the presence
is fulfilled in enjoying
the absence

• •

One becomes fearless
that fears not –
how else?
bright is the brightest
that dazzles not –
how else?

• •

The wild wind dies soon
by storming,
the breeze lasts long;
how come the former
is remembered often
the latter is often forgotten?

• •

Only by eliminating
one by one,
one approximates the One.

• •

Covering the distance twice
from here to there
one is where one was
having done nothing;
in the nature of things
all buds bloom
to the roots.

• •

The eye can see
the fool on the hill
pouring Reality into dream,
in the valley the wheel goes on
bees are busy
collecting honey
Alas! Alas!
the eye sees all –
save itself.

• •

The pot, oil and wick
mother the possible lamp
yearning to be lit,
the Light belongs to no lamp
though lit upon its tip.

• •

The thirsty river runs
to the mighty ocean
to quench the thirst
of the thirsty ocean,
while the sun awaits. . .

• •

Vulnerability opens
a thousand doors,
you are one possibility
so is God.

• •

In each peak experience
the mind merges into naught,
leaving the body free
to be what to be.

• •

I wonder
what is the development
of what?
seed of the flower
or flower of the seed
I wonder. . .

• •

Drop
dropped out
from the sea
is the sea
in the drop
is the drop
in the sea.

• •

The world of ideas
is ever changing
continuously becoming
never become.

• •

The world of appearances
is in the process
of disappearing,
to reappear
is a second step
to disappear.

• •

To be awakened
is to keep awake
and to awake further
till *this* you
and *that* you
merge.. .

• •

Your you
and my *me*
is never the same
as you and me.

• •

I am nothing more than you
you are none less than me
equal – we are not.

• •

The moment
is neither mine
nor yours
it is the moment's.

• •

Mind talks
heart speaks
soul whispers unto silence.

• •

The talker
of blessings
is unblessed.

• •

To be blessed
by this or that
is to be condemned
by that or this.

• •

Institution labels
liberation
is another story.

• •

Belief blinds
scepticism
leads nowhere.

• •

Who and which of you
longs for rendezvous
with whom and what of me?

• •

Yield your person
your place
if you want to be free
dissolve your contours –
your ends,
cross your limits
to me.

• •

Make me transcend
my time
my space
and break my border
to you.

• •

Let my
will to be –
be surrendered
into you.

• •

Discharge your duties
no matter how
take it not as fulfilments
you have far –
far to go.

• •

When you boast
you boast of your vocation
man's lot
is not limited to vocation
vocation is an entertaining
escape.

• •

To find
some meaning in life
is to give one to it
and find
that it is meaningless.

• •

Lose yourself
and find.

• •

Deny *me* not
deny *you* not
deny *it* not
for
denial establishes
the otherness
I am not other, second
in love with you.

• •

I am in union
or I AM not.

• •

Measure me not
with a given yardstick –
a scale invented
by a clever mind
I am too little
or too big
to be fitted in.

• •

The continuum of the pull
of the »Hara«
a subtle suggestion
of you in me.

• •

I am lost in you
to find
to discover
to realize myself.

• •

You there are
something – anything
everything – nothing
me – here – is
only me
let me reach out to you
in multiplicity.

• •

Take your hand
away
from my hand
I will be
more near to you
that you and me
know no distance.

• •

Assertive – myself
yourself, anyself
even nonself
is separative
feel me
flow into you
now – and timelessly.

• •

Actions correspond reactions
stand clear
transparent and perforated
as non-body
so that the wind of confusion
passes through you
in vain.

• •

You are
the knower in me
how can the knower
be known?
you are
the doer in me
how can the doer
be done?
my lips
kissed
my lips.

• •

In vain was
the arduous labour
of keeping myself
as me
let the fever of my soul
pass to you.

• •

Know yourself
not by comparison
for
you will only know
how to compare
two.

• •

You *are*
not because of
what you *are not,*
you simply *are.*
this simple of you
is the whole
of the whole,
sense it
beyond senses.

• •

Let things happen
in silence and awareness
do not ask me to think
»intellectual jugglery –
a hindrance«
else I will stand
in between
you and me
for – knowing is not becoming
and becoming is not being.

• •

»Emotional endeavour
a hindrance«
lusty – momentary
love is not a feeling
feelings fail,
feel it not
for feeling is not
the feeler and feeler
is not the being.

• •

You have been
too long
hung up high
on the cross
in the show
let your hung-ups
be hung up high
on the cross
in the show
and slide down
to me,
I am a grain
of earth
wetted by your
lonely tear.

• •

I, thc unknown
you, the inconceived
we, beyond us
free from the bondage
of deity and devotee.

• •

The baby of situation
will play a few days
more –
so long as
time makes some sense
to it.

• •

I, which is
is cradled, nourished
by that process
the situations
the environments;
I-less, which also is,
is beyond situations
whatsoever,
womb of situation
conceived it not
succession of situations
tempered it not.

• •

Language is insufficient
colours are static
sound is time-conditioned
light is space-bound
time and space
are relativity-stricken.

• •

Sensitive and super sensitive
activities are mental-material
in the end
limited by their
dimensions and directions.

• •

Growth is another story
that will grow
which is.

• •

The man, unmanifested
is also the man
more than the man
the multiple and the divided
of the gross, subtle and
supreme.

• •

Conceive the nature
of the man,
womb is the place
of what you see,
don't see only
what you see.

• •

Man is a saint
in sleep
poet in dreams
rest is nightmare.

• •

Egg-life
self-contained
in deep meditation
egg-space
in silent communication
with all-space
should you
know the shell?
I will meet you
at shell-level
should you
know the space?
I will meet you
at space-level.

• •

The tree in the seed
is also the tree
breathing, waiting
in silence and stillness
with folded hands
to manifest.

• •

The tree
grown out from the seed
is also the tree
waving and waiting
with open arms
to receive
whatever is given.

• •

See the seed
beyond the seed
the potential flower
in-deed.

• •

The stone unrevealed
is also the stone –
reject it as dead
or accept it as life
it will become so,
forget it
it will be forgotten.

• •

Stone-life
dcvoid of movement –
is still,
that is the only movement
the stillness
the action
in inaction
mobile stillness.

• •

Who could wait
till the moment
of action?

• •

Winds are winds
from north or south
from east or west,
cool or blazing
surrendering – dissolving
their identity – individuality
into each other
yet retaining all
in the *all-space*
independent of
directions and dimensions
whatsoever –
so are you and me
and all
the one is free
from any second
yet it is all.

• •

Clouds are clouds
any hue any form
surrendering – dissolving
their identity – personality
into each other
yet retaining all
in the *all-space*
so are you and me
and all
the one is free
from any second
yet it is all.

• •

The wind and the cloud
in the ecstasy
of their orgasm
cease to be
the wind and the cloud.

• •

Contraction is the rule
to enjoy
expansion –
at nobody's cost.

• •

The way is a game to play
the Truth comes home
reveals the real face
that was already the case.

• •

The conquest completes
in the *non-become* surrender,
or to become
is to become false
to be is just to be.

• •

The seeker seeks to merge
the merger does nothing –
nothing at all.

• •

In Her cave
at his core
the sage is at home
now *here* or *there*
bother him no more.

• •

Seven Spheres

The Earth is pregnant
with unearthiness.

The Water first flows
to the low
then rises.

The Fire burns itself
to purify all else.

The Air is available
to the available.

The Ether is there
where matter-spirit merge.

The Mind is the mother
and the master of the elements.

The Me and the Mind
can interpenetrate
the Whole.

• •

She is the Key

The dawn: a drop of ecstasy
of the night,
a woman's gentle sigh
spread across the sky.

She smiles:
embracing the horizon,
He wakes up under the open sky.

She laughs:
echoes into trance,
He dances:
upon the warm-wet ground.

She breathes
the fragrance of the naked fog,
He listens
to the melody of the virgin mist.

She whispers
the warm-wet secret
unto the earth,
He sleeps upon his dream
in the cosy ditch.

She touches. . .
the warm-wet secret unfolds,
He kisses
the balmy horizon blushes.

Her tongue
feels much says less,
His fingers caress the dawn
a drop of ecstasy drop
into the dusk.

• •

THE DOT
and
the dots

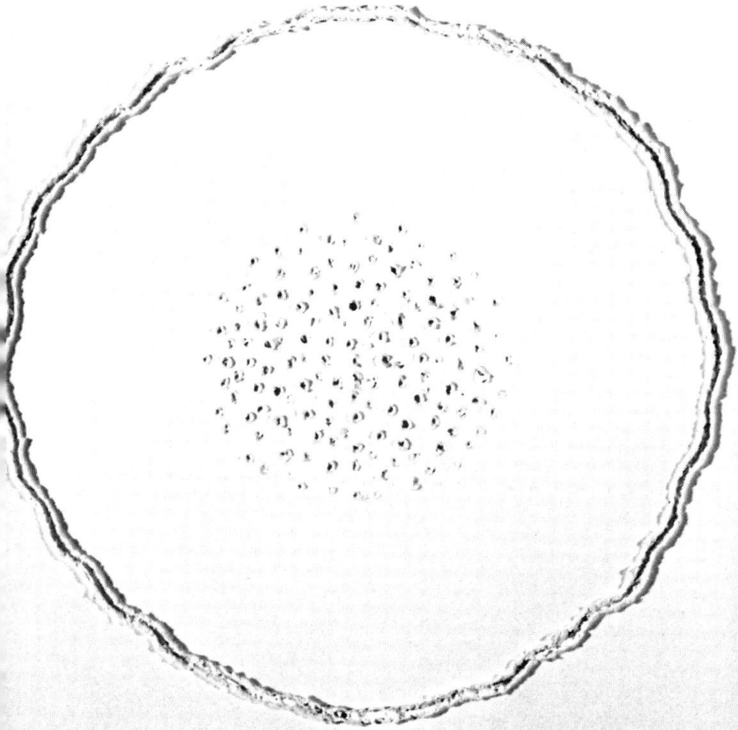

I am a dot
born out of the Dot
passing by the dots
dying into the Dot.

I am a dot
in the dot
free from dot iness.

I am a dot
in the seed of the sea,
the seed of the seeds.

I am a dot
riding a ripple
on the vast waters.

I am a dot
in the space
among the galaxies.

I am a dot
of darkness
in the dark space –
unidentified.

I am a dot
in the midnight-sun
in the arctic mysteries.

I am a dot
in the heart of ice-crystal
times old
in the antarctic mysteries.

I am a dot
following or followed by
the northern lights.

I am a dot
of light
in the light of lights.

I am a dot
in the sigh of the frustrated
in the sob of the forlorn
in the cry of the desperate.

I am a dot
of consciousness
in the waking, dreaming
and dreamless sleep.

I am a dot
on the tip
of the creator's pen.

I am a dot
in the dew-drop
on the tip of
the morning grass-blade.

I am a dot
in the dance
of the ova and sperma.

I am a dot
in the seed
in the womb of the mother.
I am a dot
in the becoming
and the being.

I am a dot
in the bound
and the unbound.

I am a dot
in the sound
unstruck.

I am a dot
in the silence
of the wise.

I am a dot
in the full, emptying itself,
in the void, filling itself.

I am a dot
of awareness
in the awakened.

I am a dot
in the animate
and the inanimate.

I am a dot
in the mindfulness
and the mindlessness.

I am a dot
in the exhalation
and inhalation
of the yogi.

I am a dot
in the drop of ecstasy
of the orgasm

I am a dot
in the drop
that ascends.

I am a dot
in the dot
that transcends.

I am a dot
of the dot
in »AUM«

I am a dot
of lust
in the longing.

I am a dot
in the chosen
and the choiceless
awareness.

I am a dot
in the profane
and the profound.

I am a dot
in the speck of dust
covering the cosmos.

I am a dot
in the obvious absurd
and the mystic befooled.

I am a dot
of fornication
between cell and cell.

I am a dot
in the pain
pregnant with pleasure
and vice versa.

I am a dot
of love
among the lips
of the lovers.

I am a dot
in the moving
that runs to the halt.

I am a dot
in the sun spent up –
the Black Hole.

I am dot
of devotion
in the deity
and devotee.
I am a dot
in the thirst of the water
– the water of waters.

I am a dot
in the disillusioned
looking for illusions.

I am a dot
of trust
in the satiated.

I am a dot
in the paradox
only a logical lie.

I am a dot
in the corporal
and the transcendental
at once.

I am a dot
in the invocations
and incantations.

I am a dot
in the pain of loneliness
and the conflict of
togetherness.
I am a dot
in the extraordinary
robed in the ordinary

I am a dot
in the enlightened
groping in the dark.

I am a dot
in the orgastic ecstasy
so spiritual
and so mundane
at once.

I am a dot
in the banal and bizarre
carrying the supreme.

I am a dot
in the naked flesh
of the flame
burning eh! enlightening.

I am a dot
in the light
in the shadow
in the caster
and the surface.

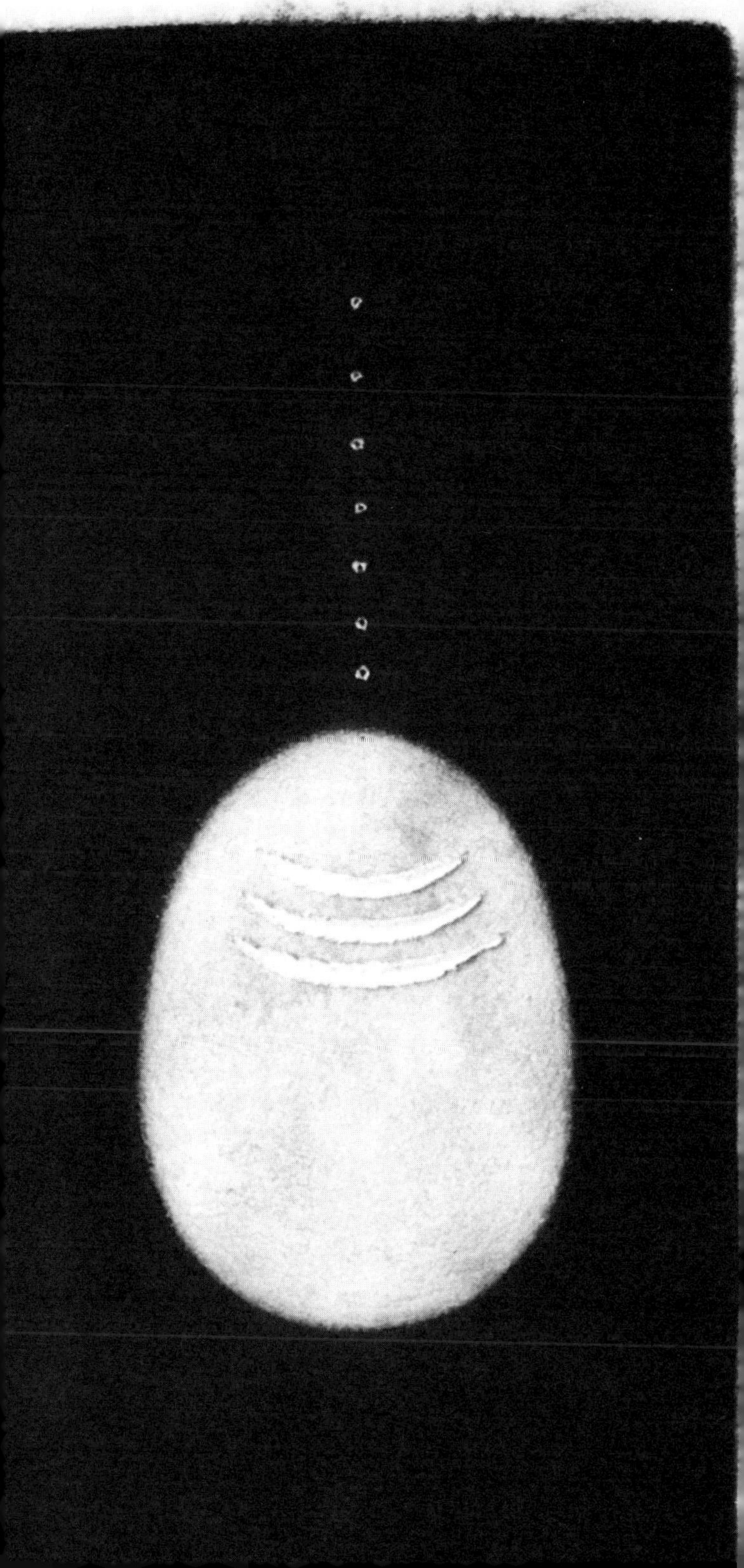

Sohan Qadri - *Wonderstand.*

No doubt, Qadri reveals his capacity for presenting themes marked by prophetic and sublime quality conveying an overwhelming interest and deep import to an individual soul. Such pregnant meditations and concise observations will cling to the memory. For example:

The answer dances when
the questioner dies in the question.

The only courage is
to watch and witness
the false face fall.

Know thy feet twice,
retreat a step to know thyself.

The talker of blessings
is unblessed.

(p. 13, 21, 35)

In all these aphoristic quotations, we notice Qadri's breadth of intellect. *Wonderstand* has very high qualities of proverbial expressions written with great precision and clarity.

Sohan Qadri's eyes are fixed upon the sober enquiry of truth, and he has relied on being able to investigate his deepest intensities in quest for epiphanies.

Wonderstand is the poetic „exhibition of psychiatry at work". The author has pondered deeply over 'all this unintelligible world (Wordsworth, Tintern Abbey), and probed sincerely in the history of his own mind.

This wisdom seems to have solved 'the burthen of the mystery' in such solemn lines:

The conquest completes
in the non-become surrender,
for to become
is to become false
to be is just to be. (p. 49)

I am a dot
in the silence
of the wise. (p. 57)

Qadri describing himself as "a dot \ in the silence" leaves no doubt in my mind that he is influenced by Nada yoga and techniques of meditation emphasizing the great significance of „a dot" or pause between inhaling and exhaling the breath.

Santosh Kumar

Extract of an article in the magazine
Critical Essays, Cyberbit.